My brother is different

By Louise Gorrod

Illustrations by Beccy Carver

The National Autistic Society

First published 1997
by The National Autistic Society
393 City Road
London EC1V 1NG
Email: nas@nas.org.uk
www.autism.org.uk

ISBN 978 1 899280 5 06

Reprinted and updated 2001, 2004, 2007 and 2011.

Text (c) Louise Gorrod 1997
Illustration (c) The National Autistic Society 1997.

Designed CottierSidaway

For Jemma & Jade

**My brother
is different.**

**Let me show you
what I mean.....**

If I am playing a game on the floor.....

... my brother tramples all over it.

This is because he doesn't know how to play games. (Even if I explain them to him.)

When we play rough and tumble, my brother sometimes gets so excited...

... that he bites or hits me.

This is because he can't control how he feels.

Sometimes when I talk to my brother...

... he ignores me.

This is because he doesn't always understand what I am saying.

Sometimes, if he is playing, he doesn't hear or see anything else.

When I behave badly I get told off...

... but my brother doesn't.
This sometimes seems unfair.

Mum says this is because I know when I am being naughty but my brother doesn't.

At mealtimes...

... my brother can't sit still.

This is because he needs lots of space and he gets upset if situations (like mealtimes) get too difficult for him.

We have locks on all our inside doors and windows...

... because my brother might try to run or jump out.

This is because he doesn't know when things are dangerous.

When we go shopping my brother screams and makes loud noises.

People stare and talk about us but...

...they do not know my brother can't
talk like me.

MY BROTHER IS DIFFERENT

When he plays with anything
he always tips it all over the floor.

He always scribbles on my drawings.

 He runs in front of the telly when I am
trying to watch it.

He can't play with other children.

16

It's unsafe for him to be let out of his pushchair.

He laughs when I am upset (because he doesn't always know what I am feeling).

He 'signs' because he does not know many words.

He will be in nappies for a long time.

MY BROTHER IS AUTISTIC

What I can do is....

... make sure he doesn't do anything
to hurt himself.
Not shout at him or smack him.
Leave him when he wants to be on his own.

I can...

... cuddle him when he comes to me.
Smile at him when he looks at me.
Read him a book when he brings one to me.
Tickle him when we play rough and tumble.
Try to understand.

BUT MOST OF ALL....

... love him.

Always.